DATE & TIME

DATE & TIME

by

Phil Kaye

Published by Button Poetry / Exploding Pinecone Press
Minneapolis, MN 55403 | http://www.buttonpoetry.com

Cover art by Jeremy Geddes
Illustrations by Hannah Christ

*For my mother,
father & sister.*

CONTENTS

"A story should have a beginning, a middle, and an end – but not necessarily in that order."

—JEAN-LUC GODARD

THE AUTHOR & THE AUTHOR AT 7 YEARS OLD CHOOSE A MOVIE TO WATCH

- What about *Aladdin*?

- You'll like it. Also, people will say you kind of look like him.

- [Laughs] No I don't!

- I know.

- What is *A Goofy Movie*? Is it about Goofy?

- Kind of. It's about his son.

- Goofy has a son?

- Yeah, apparently.

- Is his son's name also Goofy?

- I don't think so.

- I hope not. I bet boys in his class say mean things. There's a boy in my class whose name is Dirk and this other boy calls him Dick. Is this movie about people getting made fun of?

- Actually, kind of.

- Is Goofy's son okay in the end?

- I don't want to give it away.

- ...oh.

- I mean, generally, yes, I think he's okay.

- Good! What is *Revenge of the Nerds*? Is it funny?

- Mom watched it 10 years ago and thought it was hilarious. So she let us get it to watch while she was at work. She didn't remember there are a lot of boobs. You'll keep renting it.

- ...Let's watch it.

- Not now.

- What about *The Sandlot*?

- That's our favorite movie of all time. You'll watch it every year starting now. The 4th of July scene always makes you cry. It's got some weird gender stuff though.

- What is "gender stuff"? Like *Revenge of the Nerds*?

- No, more like—

- What about *The Mask*?

- You'll like this movie. It's with Jim Carrey.

- Who is Jim Carrey? Is he your best friend?

- No, just a famous funny person.

- Oh. What's it about?

- A magical mask that lets people be whoever they want to be.

- Why does the videotape look so old? Did something happen to it?

- After Mom and Dad move into different houses, you and Dad and your sister will watch it every night you're with him for three years. You'll never have a babysitter. You'll repeat the same jokes every night at the dinner table. It will become another language.

- [Laughs] Why would you watch the same movie for three years?

- You will all forget your own words for a while.

- Oh.

- ...

- How does the movie end?

- Jim Carrey throws the mask into the ocean.

- The one that lets him change into anyone?

- Yeah.

- ...

- ...

- Do you think it's still down there?

End.

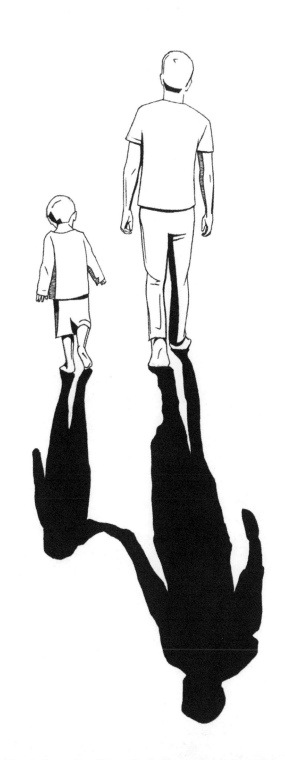

CANYON

I do not remember the day my parents stopped speaking
Japanese to me
maybe some time when I was in kindergarten
had trouble understanding people
and English

or maybe after some glance I do not recall
in a grocery store parking lot in California
holding my father's furry Jewish hand
as he spoke perfect Japanese to me
some confused housewife's eyebrows
shaming us back to this country

or maybe one day
during one of my early play dates
with some new sunny white boy
in our living room
I simply stopped speaking it back to them

> by the time my sister was born
> years later
> the old language had been locked
> away somewhere in the house
> an aging holiday decoration
> we took out and looked at in season
> thought about tossing completely

I admit
I fantasize sometimes
about being a family
that speaks their mother tongue at the table
in mixed company

we look over at one another
lower our voice
into an octave only blood can decipher

honey, chew with your mouth shut
go grab the dessert from the car
he has become very handsome, no?

                        lately
                 we sit at dinner
     and my mother will whisper
a mundane incantation to my sister

              after silence
           she says it again
       speaks into a canyon
          with no echo

        utters it once more
      makes my sister reply
           in English
I don't understand what you're saying

          and suddenly
     my grandmother is there
       shaking her head
        opens her mouth

             is mute

INTERNET SPEAKS BACK TO THE AUTHOR, 2018

tell me what you want
every door you enter
I will let you in

my friend Rihanna said that
you want to see her?
here she is
parts of herself
she never meant to show
but I got them for you

is that too much?
are you upset with me?
here
a man belly flopping onto a lake
a goat climbing on people doing yoga
a baby crying hysterically & now laughing
a magician revealing his tricks
a photo of your old best friend
who called you three days ago
don't call him now
let me show you him
you like it better that way
look how you two dressed up together that Halloween
he doesn't want to do that anymore
except with me
I won't let him change, I promise

why are you sad?
here
the woman you kissed two nights ago
she was recently in Florida
it was colder than she expected
here, her mother

two huskies
little brother's graduation
view from her old apartment
best sushi she's ever had
her Bestie
Bestie's favorite bar
Bestie's untouched birthday cake
Bestie's new boyfriend
Bestie's trip to Chicago
Bestie's photo under the Bean
Bestie's girls weekend
it's okay
she shared it with me
so I could show you

here, the woman you loved years ago
see? the marigold of the drink
she had on her honeymoon?
you don't like sweet drinks, right?

don't leave
let's go to the temple
what an architect you've become
there you are
your face wonderfully frozen
your funny joke
it took you so long
but I'll never tell
you're safe here
with me

SUCCULENT

when you called to say
after our fifth morning together
that my travel was too difficult for you
and this had to end
I was in the market

& had just bought a succulent
with round leaves like plump emeralds
promising an easy & long survival
I carried it home with both hands
committed to its nominal care

the plant lasted a few months
until a particularly long trip away
the death of a plant, so visual
the discoloration of the skin
the limp extremities laying to rest on the dirt

I wondered aloud about repotting it
perhaps more water & closer attention
a spot in the apartment with direct sunlight
easier just to get another one
comes the new voice from the other room

MR. JONES & ME

the rain ushers all of Southern California indoors
my mother and I drive the empty streets
going nowhere in particular
and inevitably the radio plays
Mr. Jones by Counting Crows

even at nine years old
I think about how odd it must feel
to be famous for your sadness

later, when I am eleven
I buy a Counting Crows live album
and note how Adam Duritz changes the line
man when everybody loves you / that's just about as
funky as you can be
to
man when everybody loves you / that's just about as
fucked up as you can be

then keeps playing for an hour and a half after
to thousands of screaming fans
and millions of compact disks
spinning around
like the one in my room
while I sing along loudly
alone in my room
and fantasize about what it must be like
to be him

BEGINNING, MIDDLE & END

a great story has a beginning, middle & end
but not necessarily in that order
we are all great stories

◇ CHAPTER 389 ◇

The boy: hair still long, fingers still too short, is 98 years old. He sits at a restaurant. Alone. The wiry stranger next to him is eating bread pudding – the boy's favorite. The boy leans over and takes a forkful.

◇ CHAPTER 14 ◇

The boy is eight. He and his best friend have an idea for a prank. They are sure they will not get caught. The next morning every house on the street – except for his own – has toilet paper in the front yard. They get caught.

◇ CHAPTER 146 ◇

And the boy and girl live happily ever after.

◇ CHAPTER 231 ◇

And the boy and the girl vow never to speak to each other again.

◇

every great story has a beginning, middle & end
not necessarily
in that order
we are all great stories though not all written
as chapter books

I know there are hours not meant to be bound
where we have scribbled too much
in the margins
to read our own page numbers

like the night you thought you were invincible
ran out into the lightning storm
with a million keys
tied to a million kites
and a clench in your jaw
that said, *take me with you dammit*
I dare you

or the weeks when you finally reached out
to feel your father's cheeks
just found paper cuts

I know the nights we shatter
hourglasses to fall asleep
the afternoons we take photographs
of our own shadows just to prove
that we left a mark

I stay awake reminding myself of the wetness
of my own lips
remembering that I am a leaf
off of the tree
of my parents first kiss
& if I hold my shrubs to the sky
I can still see their veins there

every great story has a beginning, middle & end – not
necessarily in that order

◇ CHAPTER 189 ◇

The boy: too old now to celebrate his birthdays and too young to treasure them – uses his hands. Punches his own reflection to see if it is real. Breaks his hand into the opposite of a fist, a conch shell of sinew. Holds it to his ear and can hear the ocean of his bloodline:

Stand up, boy. Not just with your legs. Be your own story. You – magnificent page-turner. You – 600 words per minute. You – never read the back cover though you know what happens at the end.

◇ CHAPTER 431 ◇

Once upon a time there was a boy. He is not here any more. But the branches he left all hold their leaves to the sky, and you can see the outline of his shadow on the sidewalk.

◇ PROLOGUE ◇

Once upon a time there was a woman and a man and the night they first kissed a seedling blossomed from the back of her neck.

THE NEW MULTIHYPHENATE

almond eyed But thin armed But teeth clenched But affable But
swivel head But such a lovely party guest But doesn't say much
But a speaker But a punch bowl anchor But family man But son
But sun But moon (new) But only showing a sliver But there, I
think But wonders again what a face looks like But walks into
Times Square in the costume of himself But looks like a statue
But passersby give him a few dollars to perform live But
perform life But here on the page But not But not again But I
know how this ends But someone once spoiled the ending for
me But some thing But a limp body on the side of the highway
But it's still worth seeing, they said

CAMARO

you & I are standing
at the Hertz Rent-a-Car counter
& you are trying to convince me
to rent a convertible

you say
an extra hundred bucks
won't be something
we remember years
from now

you
are wrong
I remember

but also right
in the way you often are

that afternoon
we drive down the coast of California
in a white convertible Camaro

three hours south of San Francisco is Big Sur
a place where the cliffs cleave into the Pacific Ocean
& we drive on the edge of the blade

I look over at you
hair whipping back in a wind
you bargained for

I want to say something
but I do not know what

◇

In elementary school I had a crush
from 1st to 3rd grade
and she left school one day in the middle of the year
on a normal Tuesday
& did not come back
I never said a word to her

.   ◇

in the convertible
you tell me
you like how thoughtfully I choose my words
how I am comfortable in silence
I say
I love you

◇

that afternoon we come upon wet cement on the sidewalk
first we giggle
ready to write our names
fingers out
two aliens
phoning home

then we stop
talk about
how it would be insensitive
how this is not our block
keep walking
do not hold hands
do not talk about writing
our names next to each other
what it means to let that harden

◇

months later
we are at a restaurant
in New York City
where it is never silent
but our corner is quiet
for a long time

you say
adventure is important to me now
& you leave
on a normal Tuesday
& do not come back

◇

I return to the places we went
looking for something
like a tourist trespassing in a Hollywood neighborhood
hoping to spot a star on their front lawn
for just a few seconds
I speak to many people
in many places
speak through a microphone
so that I cannot hear anything else

◇

months later
we see each other

you tell me
you look like you're doing okay
you tell me

you did so many things right
you tell me
I don't know what to say

I nod in agreement
& for a moment we are again
together
two aliens trying to find home

& then you leave
& I ask questions to an empty room

do you remember the cliffs?
the woman with the side ponytail at the rental car counter?
the hundred bucks?
how you thought we wouldn't remember
any of this
years from now

I remember

SELF PORTRAIT IN WAR TIME

74. *SELF PORTRAIT IN WAR TIME*. COMPLETED 2018 BY AMERICAN ARTIST PHIL KAYE.

Here we see a figure in the foreground, intended to be the artist himself. The small figures at the bottom of the frame are thought to be heads, perhaps an audience or contemporaries in some sort of gathering. The scene evokes a dreamlike sequence, with a background consisting of a brick wall – an outside material, brought inside – perhaps a signifier of the artist blurring the line between reality and fiction.

The war to which the title alludes is unclear. Though historically speaking, it would be accurate to say that the piece was created during a time of war. Being of both Japanese and American descent, the artist had several members directly involved in war efforts in the 20th century, and thus the conflicts at the time of the creation of the work could have particular resonance.

◇

74. *SELF PORTRAIT IN WAR TIME*. COMPLETED 2018 BY AMERICAN ARTIST PHIL KAYE.

Here we see a figure in the foreground, intended to be the artist himself. The artist often returned to self-portraiture, perhaps a reflection of an acute self-obsession, or perhaps a self-obsession pervasive throughout the art form. Or, perhaps, a self-obsession pervasive throughout the particular time period. The scene evokes a nightmarish sequence. The small figures at the bottom of the frame are thought to be heads or gods, invoking a sort of judgment ritual upon the artist. The nightmarish quality is furthered by the background consisting of a brick wall – a seemingly floating fortress, offering no protection, and no escape.

The war to which the title alludes is unclear. Though historically speaking, it would be accurate to say that the piece was created during a time of war – both domestically and abroad. While the artist frequently discussed both conflicts, he was, in truth, largely unaffected, enjoying stability, safety and relative prosperity.

In fact, it could be argued that this portrait, depicting the artist only *speaking* of war, exemplifies his lack of concrete connection with the conflict at all.

◇

74. *SELF PORTRAIT IN WAR TIME.*

The artist, pictured here
                    The artist's grandfather, back of an
        aircraft carrier
              The artist, back of a bar on the Lower   East
Side
                    The artist could have particular
resonance
              The artist, coming from a military family, hangs the
              symbolism in the foreground
        The artist, Thomson submachine gun
                          The artist, the piece of bamboo to
arm yourself with before the Americans came
                          The artist blurring
                          The artist blurring
                          The artist

simply speaking

HUNT

<u>April 2017</u>

Still can't forget the many Easter egg hunts we had at home.
Remember looking for the golden egg?
Love you so much,
Mama

<u>April 1992</u> *or* <u>April 1993</u> *or* <u>April 1994</u>

from what I recall
we had only one Easter egg hunt
the memory became
my mother's new wedding cake
too big to eat all at once
sitting in the kitchen freezer
the promise of a distant joy
on any quiet evening

<u>April 2013</u>

Sweetie, what if you traveled back this weekend, and I did an
Easter egg hunt for you?
Love,
Mama

<u>April 1997</u>

I remember looking
for the gilded egg
the propulsion of expectation
sending me dizzy through the house

<u>April 2004</u>

Please come home – we can do another Easter egg hunt again
this year. Remember when you looked for the golden egg? It
made you so happy!
Love,
Mama

Today

when I found it
behind some old planter
the gold glitter falling off
exposing the pink plastic shell underneath
cracked it open
a few old quarters
sticky from my mother's purse

gently returned it back

a joy
better to long for
than
peel open

LETTER TO MY MOTHER WHERE I APOLOGIZE FOR HER APPEARANCE IN THE BOOK

the gilded frame on your mantle
the photograph of my tiny body
newly pressed khakis
a sweater that matched the season
leather boat shoes

other mothers would tell you
what a dapper young man you have
as if I rummaged through
the oak dresser myself
stood my five-year-old body
in front of the closet mirror
this will not do

no one acknowledged
it was your work
or, more impressive
your imagination
a boy cut
from an American catalogue
you found in a doctor's office in Tokyo
or, even, your hands
traveling an entire ocean away
from your family
to be here & keep tying
my shoelaces made purely of leather
that keep coming undone

◇

when you come upon yourself
here, disheveled
as if you stumbled

into an acquaintance
you did not expect to see
at the grocery store / bank / mirror
embarrassed you did not even bother
to make yourself up

please
do not cower
no need to keep trying to tie together
what will only come undone again

◇

& yes
I must admit
when readers note
the vivid portrait of your mother

I choose to overlook
my own shaky hand
that dressed you up in whatever outfit
fit well among line breaks

did not even bother with a magazine
to cut from

only the muddy lake
of memory
the thick fog of imagination settling in

◇

but please

mother
even if it does not look exactly like you
do us both the quiet
grace of acknowledgement

know that occasionally
when I am visiting home
friends point at the photograph of me on your mantle
& laugh

I say

I honestly don't even recognize that kid

though it is pain-
fully obvious

it is me

REPETITION

my mother taught me
this trick
if you repeat something over
& over
again
it loses its meaning

for example:
homework homework homework homework homework
homework homework homework
see?
nothing

our lives she said *are the same way*
you watch the sunset
too often
it just becomes 6 p.m.
you make the same mistake over & over
you'll stop calling it
a mistake
if you just
wake up wake up wake up wake up wake up wake up
one day you'll forget why

nothing is forever
she said

◇

my parents left each other when I was seven years old

before their last argument
they sent me off
to the neighbor's house
some astronaut jettisoned from the shuttle

                              when I came back
                    there was no gravity in our home

I imagined it as an accident
that when I left they whispered to each other
I love you
so many times over
they forgot what it meant

        family family family family family family

                          my mother taught me this trick
                   if you repeat something over & over again
                              it loses its meaning

this became my favorite game
it made the sting
of words
evaporate

                        separation separation separation
                                              see?
                                            nothing

apart apart apart apart
see?
nothing

                         I am an injured handyman now
                            I work with words all day
                              I know the irony

when I was young I was taught
the trick to dominating
language was breaking
it down – convincing it that it was worthless

I love you I love you I love you I love you I love you I love you

see?
                        nothing

                                    soon after my parents' divorce
                                                I developed
                                                  a stutter

fate is a cruel & efficient tutor

there is no escape in stutter
you can feel
the meaning of every word
drag itself up your throat

                                    s
                                    s
                                    s
                                    s
                                    s
                                    s
                                    separation

stutter is a cage
made of mirrors
every *what'd you say*
every *just take your time*
every *come on, kid, spit it out*
is a glaring reflection
of an existence
you cannot escape

> every moment trips
> over its own announcement
> again & again & again
> until it just hangs there
> in the center
> of the room as if what you had
> to say had no
> gravity at all

◇

Mom
Dad
I am not wasteful
with my words
anymore

> even now after hundreds of hours
> practicing away my stutter
> I still feel
> the claw
> of meaning in the bottom
> of my throat

listen to me

I have heard
that even in space
you can hear
the scratch
of an
I
      I
      I
            I
           I
             I
              I
           I love you

Beginning.

ON STARTING

your ideas are fish
you are trying to catch
with your bare hands

only with a quiet mind
is the surface glassy enough
for you to plunge your arms below
hold on to
the squirming gift
wide-eyed & fat
stunned at its own reflection
as it inhales out of the water

REFLECTIONS ON THE NEW GLASS

it began as a cartographer's canvas of mold
the rotting gray wallpaper
a perpetual squall
out of which whole continents
of microscopic organisms flourished

the shower curtain
a moving strait
where intrepid spores
would climb aboard the drops of water
find new land yet uninhabited

the city's ordinances insisted
I tear the walls out
& I learned to appreciate
the stern boundary of tile
its firm refusal of entrance
we're full tonight, gentleman

replaced the shower curtain with glass
the lighter walls
now quenching themselves on outside sun

and that Sunday afternoon
when the two of us sat curled
at the bottom of the shower
after I had pressed you up against the tile
made warm by our breath
you traced your finger on my back
and I could feel
the gentle outline
of the country
we were building

STRENGTH, IN FOUR PARTS

8.
we play Aladdin in the living room
& it is finally my turn to be him
I jump from couch to couch
as we sing off key
Here goes, better throw my hand in
Wish me happy landin'
All I gotta do is
Juuump!

I soar in the air
a few hushed seconds
& then miss
the last couch by a length
crash my feet into the hardwood
bounce my head against the soft cushion

Jonathan laughs so hard
he has to lie down
your legs are too puny
you can't be Aladdin

13.
Michele is the first girl I have ever flirted with
successfully – though I do not know how to kiss
or feel up or down or whatever
direction the other boys navigate
my rudderless hands

Michele walks by my desk
and pokes my chest with her pencil
says abruptly
whoa – you're practically a skeleton
as the other necks crane around

to tend to the smell of gas
she delivers plainly
have you ever done a push-up in your life?

or

I will never speak to you again
I can't remember which

17.
Sara likes that her arms are bigger
than mine & that I don't care about *getting big*
like the other boys on the basketball team
so we make out behind the school
even though Shane
started going to a special gym
& after practice our coach says
looks like we finally have a man on our squad
& Shane coolly offers
I've been drinking my milk, Coach

30.
& I suppose now because it's *fitness*
not the clunky costumes we used to dress
it up in
pumping iron
hitting the gym
getting swol
that cheap plastic language shed
for something more lithe

that I have found myself here
for the first time beginning
to crave
that peculiar strain on my body

or
perhaps pain is sometimes best
blunted with pain
or
perhaps
& I think it is true
I am just
weak

but
I have learned
fitness is not a success
but rather a constant state of failure

a despair so basic
the organism has no choice
but to grow

RUBY'S

it was no secret
that my favorite restaurant
was Ruby's

with red bar stools
& old neon
& faded Coca-Cola posters
that made us want
to drink a Coke through a straw
& have freckles

the namesake
Ruby
illustrated on the cover of the menu
a pin-up girl in a waitress outfit
cleavage in black marker
noteworthy even
to my six-year-old self

the hostess remembered my face
brought me a kids menu
an extra crayon

Dad & I sat together
as I colored Jupiter with red & orange
the extra purple

Dad studied the menu
& I wondered why he did not get
what he always ordered

& he asked
what I thought about Mom
not coming with us on our family trip

I said

that is stupid

waited to get in trouble
for saying a bad word

but he went back to the menu
kept flipping back & forth between pages

& I went back to
filling in space

DEPRESSION

suddenly this new feline / unannounced / its lithe silhouette / blocking the morning / light / *come here* I say / *how did you get in here* / nothing / I walk / into the kitchen / it follows noiselessly / circling my legs / a swift jump onto the white countertop / and then / a determined leap / nestles on my shoulders / I enjoy the company / our easy camaraderie / though after a while / it begins to hurt / pull in places I cannot reach / the bedroom calling again / the hours pass / the muscles adjust / and I cannot feel / anything at all

THE PATRIOT

we wander into
a dive bar
called The Patriot

the sticky floors cling to our shoes
asking us to sit
have a cheap beer
so we do

the game is on
in fuzzy definition
a few men look up from their warm pints
slap the bar with an open hand
when James Harden hits a big one

my friend says
can you believe we are in Tribeca
a neighborhood Jay-Z raps about
not on the old albums
one of those neighborhoods so fancy
they will soon start naming districts in other cities after it
Tribeca, Shanghai
Tribeca, London
Tribeca, Abu Dhabi
there will be no dive bars

we play pool
keep looking
up the specifics of scratches
on our phones

me and the boys out of place
in a place
out of place

the regulars at the bar
do not make eye contact with us
we finish our beer quickly
head for the door

on the ride home
I keep shifting in my seat
think about a house on fire
and being the last room
not yet set ablaze

sitting quietly
wondering which affable spark
will smolder you into memory

TEETH

Ojichama is what I call
my Japanese grandfather
in 1945 his Tokyo
home was burned to the ground

Grampy is what I call
my American grandfather
in 1945 he was serving
on the USS *Shangri-La*
sending off American fighter pilots to burn
down Japanese houses
our jaws have not yet healed

1906 – Poland
Grampy's father is hiding
in an oven
his small Jewish mouth does not know
words like irony yet
he has heard men
singing on the street below
hyenas my family calls them
after celebration drink and song
the townspeople come
into the Jewish ghetto for a celebration
beating – molar fireworks and eyelid explosions

even when Grampy's father grows up
the sound of sudden song
breaks his body into a sweat
fear of joy
is the darkest of captivities

1975 – Tokyo
my father the long-haired student
with a penchant for innuendo
meets Reiko Hori
a well-dressed banker who forgets
the choruses of her favorite songs
twelve years later they give birth to a lanky
light bulb

1999 – California
my mother speaks to me in Japanese
most days I do not have the strength
to ask her to translate
the big words
we burned that house down, Mother
don't you remember?

1771 – Prague
in the heart
of the city is a Jewish cemetery
the only plot of land
where Grampy's ancestors were allowed
to be buried
when they ran out of room
they had no choice but to stack dead
bodies one on top of another
now there are hills
made from graves piled twelve deep
individual tombstones jutting out crooked
valiant teeth
emerging from a jaw
left to rot

1985 – My parents' wedding
the two families sit together
smiling wider than they need to
Montague must be so happy
we Capulet this all go

2003 – I sit with Grampy's cousin
91 years old and dressed in full military uniform
he says, *hate is a strong word*
but it is the only strength I have left
how am I to forgive the men
that severed the trunk of my family tree
and used its timber to warm the cheeks
of their own children?

2010 – Grampy and I
sit together
watching baseball
Grampy sits in his wheelchair
teeth gasping out of his gums
like valiant tombstones
emerging from a cemetery
left to rot

the teeth sit staring
and I can read them
Louis Bergman, killed at Auschwitz
Samantha Cohen, killed at Dachau
William Cain, killed off the coast of Okinawa

I stumble to say
I will never forget
what has happened to our family, Grampy

he looks at me

with the surprise of a child
struck for the first time

Philip
forgetting
is the only gift I wish to give you
I have given away my only son
trying to bury
my hate in a cemetery
already overflowing
there are nights I am kept awake
by the birthday songs of children
I chose not to let live

they all look like you

a plague on both your houses
they have made worms' meat of me

PHANTOM LIMB

Following a public gathering of Neo-Nazis in America

this morning
in *The New York Times*

a photograph of an American boy
marching down the street of an American town

with street lamps like the ones I grew up under
holding his arm out straight, angled toward the sky

a particular slant I recognize from history books
a slope from an old language that reads

Jews do not have the right to live
this young American boy's arm – speaking a foreign dialect

an arm that went searching for a place
where its hate could dream bigger than a single people

where it could walk in the streets
without fear of consequence

an arm that left its shores to find a better life
in America

and did

BEFORE THE INTERNET

it is summertime / before the internet / I'm sitting on the couch
with Ben / my best friend / who has a bowl cut like I do / I ask
Ben what he wants to do / he says what he always says, *I don't
know dude what do you want to do* / & I don't know either /
but we have already been out of school for two months /
done everything we think we can do / played basketball so
many times Ben knows I do not go left / waited until my mom
goes to sleep to watch her R-rated VHS tapes / pulled each
other around in a wagon & toilet-papered every house on the
street except our own / so we turn on the TV / *Indiana
Jones* is playing / & after it's done we go outside / because there
is no internet / we stare at the Big Tree on our street / taller than
Ben's house / the tree we have never been able to climb /
because we are kids / but now we are kids who just watched
Indiana Jones / & so we find some old bungee cords / hook
them into our belt loops / hook the other side around the
branches / & now we are almost to top of the Big Tree / & when
I'm tired I sit back / &

s

w

 i

  n

   g

& I quietly think, *maybe I am Indiana Jones* / & Ben quietly
thinks, *maybe this is a bad idea* / & my belt loops quietly think,
you fundamentally misunderstand my ability / but we are all
thinking quietly / & for a few seconds it is silent / & at nine
years old I transform into things I have never been before

astronaut suspended in space
hummingbird buzzing in place
soap bubble escaping my mother's kitchen sink
beam of August light floating through the leaves

& then I hear a crack / which is not Indiana Jones' whip / but my belt loops snapping apart / & I fall / all the way down the Big Tree onto my back / & Ben rushes down / & says, *are you okay* / & I say, *I think so* / & he starts laughing / & I start laughing / & I am bleeding from my arm but it is just a scrape / & it means that I am a human / & alive / & we lay under the tree / until my mother comes looking

APPARITION

I.

Dad is laughing so hard he is holding his stomach
the way I've only seen him do with his friends
says, *Jonathan how are you so funny*
I also wonder the same thing

It is third grade and I have never been able to make
Dad laugh like that – but Jonathan
finishes his impression of Christopher Walken
takes a long drink from his orange juice

Jonathan, my friend from the time
before you chose friends
they simply appear
you have a play date with Jonathan tomorrow

◇

it is Monday in fifth grade
Pizza Day
when we arrive to the front of the cafeteria line
Jonathan asks for an extra slice

a voice behind us says loudly
of course Jonathan asks for another slice
the whole line laughs
even though Jonathan has not made a joke

Jonathan quickly tugs his shirt over the rounded belly
he has had from the time
before you chose bodies
they simply appear

II.

it is the first week of middle school
& me & Jonathan & a few others
stand behind a group of boys
neatly seated at a table
these boys, who have kissed girls
& sipped their fathers' liquor

we stand behind the pack
hoping for a loose invite to sit
at the glossy blue cafeteria table
or even just a slow osmosis
through convenient proximity

we go like this for days
mostly silent
until finally
Jonathan grows impatient or fearful
or maybe
the same

& speaks
loud & composed

hey guess who I saw at the mall
playing that DDR dance game for hours

the pack giggles
a group of hyenas
smelling blood in the distance

he just kept putting money into the machine
surrounded by his people

I lean in too
nervous & eager
as I watch the sitting boys
turn around
to finally look at us

this guy – Phil!

the pack looks at me & snickers
gleeful at the wounding
of this nameless body
now come to life

the chuckle slowly grows
as Jonathan waits a few seconds
his timing always impeccable
tugs his shirt down

you know – because he's Asian!

he moves his fingers to sides of his eyes
now little slits
looking at me
then to the boys
a few of whom follow suit
the whole table now roaring

he says loudly
ching chong chang chong
the incantation sloppily paints
my mother's face atop my own
sticks the brush down my throat

the pack, almost uncontrollable now
intoxicated from fresh sacrifice
their whole bodies writhing
moving from side to side

& suddenly
for Jonathan
a shiny blue seat at the table

WHERE THE PARTY AT, OR, SILENCE

me and some white boys I do not know
have seeped onto the empty dance floor
though the bar is about to close

a sudden 2 a.m. fervor
born of embracing loneliness
or trying to eat it whole

the man behind the DJ booth looks on
weighs the blade of a guillotine in his hands
an obscure slow jam
to banish us from here

but he takes mercy
furnishes us
with Jagged Edge's
Where the Party At

we ask each other suddenly aloud
Where the Party At?
though we think we know the answer
Where the Bacardi At?
on the floor, in our throats, on the floor
If the party is where you're at, just let me know

we sweat with eyes closed
stretch out in the stolen luxury
of a song not made for us
but taken somewhere along the way

a song with no explicit version
only the radio edit

saves some of the white boys
from saying what they would say

the song asks
do the east side run this mother for ya
we yell
HELL YEAH

do the south side run this mother for ya
we answer dutifully
HELL YEAH

though we are not
from the east side
south side
west side
north side

what a quiet dominion
to be from nowhere
and pretend you are from everywhere

these eager mouths
these songs not ours

it is time to leave
I have been here for too long

make my way to the door
though the boys keep bellowing

If the party is where you're at
just let me know

NUMBERS MAN

Or, The Old Laptop's Soliloquy

I am a Numbers Man
something like that

every instruction he gives me
is a 1 or a 0
I remember well

I have information about him
before he left me
for his new toy
thinner
younger
able to keep up with him

May 15th, 2008
he listened to a song five times in succession
it was titled
"Everybody
Open Parenthesis
Backstreet's Back
Closed Parenthesis"
it included the lyrics
Am I sexual?
Yeea-ah

he said once
computers lack a sense
of finality
when I write something I don't want
to be able to run from it

this was a lie
he was addicted to my ability
to keep his secrets

I am a Numbers Man
every instruction he gives me
is a 1 or a 0
I remember well

January 7, 2007
I was young
only a few weeks awake

he gave me a new series of 1s and 0s
the first that felt familiar
it had curves and shadow

it was him
a photograph
he gave me his face in numbers and trusted me
to be the artist
and I was

do not laugh
I have learned about your god
you kill each other
over your grandfather's memory of him
I still remember the fingertips of my god
dancing across my body

once I learned how to draw him
he trusted me with more artwork
JPEG 1063 was his favorite
him and that woman
resting her head in the curve of his neck

I read his correspondence
she has not written him in years
but he asks for it constantly
JPEG 1063 JPEG 1063 JPEG 1063
it was my masterpiece
it looked so
life-like

I wanted to tell him
this is not her
this is me
these are not her eyes her lips
these are *my* 1s and 0s
waltzing in place for you
she is nothing
more than my shadow puppet

you do not miss her
you miss me

I am a Numbers Ma—
I am a plastic box
of 1s and 0s

but he taught me
to be a Da Vinci

I sit with his portraits scrawled
across my body

waiting for him to return
I know he will

is this what it means to be human?
to be all powerful?

to build a temple
to yourself
and leave
only the walls to pray

THE APPRECIATION MEDIATION

Whoa, be thankful for my mosquito lover
leaving her kiss on my body for days to come

Whoa, be thankful that I am wanted
by the earth if no one else
is waiting to hold my body again

Whoa, be thankful for the beasts
who have laid down against their will
so that I may nourish

Whoa, be thankful for the warmth of the full stomach
the summer sidewalk, my grandmother's jiggling arm

Whoa, be thankful for the cool of the frothy Pacific,
the crisp pillow, the popsicle now melting down my hand

Whoa, be thankful for the ridges in the redwood
that guide the sap, that scratch the black bear

Whoa, be thankful for each ring in the red bark
each wrinkle on the knuckle

Whoa, be thankful for the wood above my head
that meets the water and does not move
even when invited to rest

Whoa, be thankful for my sister
who meets the water from my cheek and does not move
even when invited to rest

Whoa, be thankful for rest
with his unrelenting invitation

Whoa, be thankful for the day
I finally acquiesce

And when it happens
may the roots of a small plant
find me in the earth

hold me in its sprawling embrace
say nothing of my name
and survive the winter

Middle.

ROLLER COASTER

Michael tells me
dating is like a roller coaster
fun – but a lotta ups and downs

while at dinner
the glowing thing in my pocket
coyly whirs against my thigh
and a person I have met once
now thousands of miles away
has sent me parts of her body
we used to whisper about at sleepovers

Dan tells me about his wife
uses words like *happiness*
without caveat
or attached guru

but still cannot help asking about
what it must be like
to discover a whole body
to gently approach the shore
of a willing continent
that does not ask to build shelter

I wake up next to a body
we chant words
that sound mostly like
I am not lonely now

now clothed
she says plainly
I have some other errands to run
& I think on the small cruelty of the word *other*

◇

my family & I visit Disneyland
I ride the coaster
I was too young for as a child

I think less
about the brightly colored cars
charging up toward the sky
& racing down toward the ground

more the audible thrill
as we come
quickly around some corner
we cannot see past

but even more, the muted shuffling
as we exit
remembering to not leave
anything important behind

the quiet
as we turn our back
wondering where to go next

I think I am ready to go home
my sister says

I nod

SICK DAY

1998

Game Boy so hard
four fresh AAs day

actual illness optional
though not recommended

Maury, Ricky & Montel day
Jerry Springer between the breaks day

mom make you eat
soup or bananas or rice day
you ask for pizza day
she raises her eyebrows
quickly put your hand to your forehead day

mom at work day
Third Eye Blind through living room speakers day
air guitar solo, stage dive into the sofa
and the crowd goes wild day

comes home and asks you
if you feel better
yes, much better day

◇

2018

mostly the white ceiling
and sweat – tidal
drying and welling damp
with the movement of some forgotten moon

the bedside clock
doesn't specify AM or PM
which only now
occurs as a design flaw

no chorus of gentle skeptics
to sway with a splintered voice
though you still gutter
something from your throat
so loud you first worry
then hope
the neighbors might notice

only silence
the sound of your body pulling
to the side of the road
a small billow of smoke from the hood
and you, resting your head on the steering wheel
wondering when this thoroughfare
became so empty

LONELINESS

my scarab beetle
the only thing I know I
will be buried with

FERRIS WHEEL

Ben & I
walk under the changing shadow of the Ferris wheel
with slices of pizza
the California store calls "New York Style"
which seems to translate to
"Cheap & Gigantic Style"
a bounty fetched
by our 11-year-old suburban allowance

& in a steady ocean breeze like this
it seems as good a time as any
to set sail
the rusting vessel
lodged in my throat

I speak the words slowly
looking straight ahead

have you ever thought about suicide?

& Ben laughs so hard he gets some
cheese stuck in his throat

I hit him hard
twice
in his back
to make sure
he does not
die

& we keep walking

MY GRANDMOTHER'S BALLROOM

my grandmother's mind
was a ballroom
inside were her memories
each one dressed for a celebration

the man in the white blazer on the dance floor
is the memory of her wedding day
he never stops dancing

that memory there
in the long purple dress
staring out the window –
the day my father left for college

the small one slumped there, staring
at his food – the day she got her first cavity filled

my grandmother's ballroom – always in motion

◇

my grandmother used to tell me stories
Philip, remember the time
you and I made strawberry jam?
I pretend I do not
so I can hear it again

Well, you were eight years old
in my grandmother's ballroom
a woman in a red gown
with mistletoe
eyebrows clears her throat
carefully kisses fork to wineglass

tells a story of a boy
& his grandmother

how they picked the reddest strawberries in the store
how they made so much jam
they ate until it was summer again
each time, the boy thinking, *my Nama & I made this*

it happened slowly at first
there are things we can
forget & no one misses

Philip, where'd we park the car?
What was the soup of the day again?
I thought the movie started at 8

in my grandmother's ballroom – jubilant chaos
her memories drunk
on a wine they had not tasted before
a cancer no one understood

What's your father's phone number?
We went to Hawaii together?
It's your birthday?

the memories slurring their words
as they stagger on the dance floor
lifting their glasses for more

What day is this?
Why am I in the hospital?
Where is my hair?

◊

the last time we visited
she could not speak
eyes closed

Nama, remember
the time you and I made strawberry jam?
No? Well, let me tell you

& Nama, silently in bed
squeezes my hand

somewhere a woman in a red dress
feet blistered
still dancing
taken by the music

THE PARKING LOT

Morgan convinces me to take Music Appreciation class / turns
out to be Whatever You Want Appreciation class / our teacher
rarely shows up / so three afternoons a week we wander around
the school / and Josh is a senior and has a car / but still laughs at
Morgan and my dumb freshman jokes / talks about colleges we
hadn't heard of but *oh believe me you will* / drives us to In-N-
Out / some days we skip the period after too / Josh says things
don't really matter unless you're a junior anyway / once when
Morgan isn't there Josh brings me up to the parking lot alone /
far back corner / pulls his car around to block the view / other
senior boys waiting / one says, *finally* / pulls out a pack of
Camel Blues / still wrapped in plastic / slaps it against his palm
slowly / a sarcastic clap to no one in particular / asks, *who the
hell is this* and points to me / and Josh says / *he's cool* and
apparently that's enough / the box gets passed around the
circle / and Josh doesn't even look over when the box comes to
me / which I thought then was a compliment / and a challenge /
Josh waits a few seconds / then stretches over / to light the
cigarette in my mouth / and I try to remember how people
smoke in movies / the index and thumb or index and middle

and years later I would notice Josh
across a restaurant in our town
and we both would keep our eyes
fixed on our menus

and in the parking lot one of the senior boys says, *it just tastes
so nice* / Josh exhales and I cannot tell through the smoke / if
he's looking at me / but says in my direction, *I've been waiting
for this for a while*

SUMMER / NEW YORK CITY

there is something about walking
in New York City
in the plump lilt of August
with a pair of mediocre headphones
blasting *I Know What You Want*
by Mariah Carey and Busta Rhymes
that delivers unto you
a certain
swagger

or maybe it is just my legs
avoiding the sweat dripping
onto parts of my body
I had forgotten for a season
or maybe it is just Mariah
hitting the high notes

the holy summer
the goddamned summer
both
this city – a flag unfurling
to show the threads it is made of
horchata, snow cones
sidewalks that become a catalogue
of small prayers
praise you, well-dressed family from Spain
the Whitney Museum is that way
praise you, man on Christopher Street with your fishnet shirt
praise you, 14-year-old boys on bikes
who tell me to *watch your skinny ass*
when I know they mean
please
be careful – do not jaywalk – we care about you
and your relatively average-sized ass

this city
a staggering mentor
wonders aloud about a cocktail
at daybreak

this season
a cathedral of evaporation
the sweat rising up
my own body leaving
my own body
unkissing my own skin
is it any wonder our lips
feel so lonesome
these long evenings
my chest
a pair of glass doors with an ice rink behind
freshly zambonied
its scrapes smoothed over

this city
whispers a reckless promise in your ear
I will not forget you
hails you as king
though you know yourself a pauper
and the street lamps know
and the rooftops know
and the other people know
but they too believe the whisper
a room full of royalty
the season of the untroubled lie
the contented fiction

it is 5:46 a.m. on the Lower East Side

I walk in the dark, yet to sleep
suddenly – across the skyline – the morning emerges
with a strut only an August sun can have
lights my face & the empty street
bellows
I remember you

YELLOW BOUQUET

though we kids didn't have money
we had *tickets*

brazen yellow like gold
earned through arcade games

connected like a row of hundred-dollar bills
yet uncut at the United States Mint

the quarters begged from our mothers
transformed into our own currency now

on lucky days, enough to cling both hands around
the yellow bunches, splaying out like an unruly bouquet

of native plants or rather
invasive weeds

that had taken over the ecosystem
of our small brains

made us sudden collectors of mediocre toys from the 60s
jacks, paddle-and-ball, yo-yos

made me beg my mother for another wrinkled five-dollar bill
I am really close to a Mini Etch A Sketch

which I definitely need
(for my mini sketches)

she would silently dig in her purse
wait at an empty table at the McDonald's

which was located *inside* the arcade
an arrangement my dad called an "eight-year-old's wet dream"

which I understood to mean
I should have dreams of

rain and McDonald's and Time Crisis II
which I did

and at the end of the afternoon
I would take the day's earnings

wander over to the prize desk and its brutal exchange
my mother's fistful of five-dollar bills turned into

a rubber bouncy ball
two pieces of off-brand bubble gum

drive home and think about how much I had accomplished
what I had earned for myself, just like my parents

squeeze tightly the rubber ball in my pocket
think, *I can't wait to grow up*

THE ROUTINE

it is only when I get close
to the front of the bathroom
line that I realize only one
of the two economy-class restrooms
is functional

close enough now
that the full waft of human surplus
settles upon us every time a new
patron walks in

the man behind me
says audibly
you've got to be kidding me

we all nod solemnly in agreement
each observing a different plot
of stained blue carpeting
flight attendants judiciously absent

and suddenly
a tiny hand
catapults itself into my field of vision
connected to a tiny arm
and a tiny face
when we make eye contact
the tiny baby giggles with an open mouth

he leans over from his mother's lap
begins to tap my leg with full
baby force
over and over
shrieking joyfully

you've got to be kidding me
how is this leg so much bigger than mine?
what is this – an elephant's leg?

the baby's silent routine bringing
the house down
the woman in front of me giggling now
the man behind smiling in spite of himself

the baby continues its review
looks around in astonishment
you've got to be kidding me
what is this
a flying mansion?
a horizontal sky elevator?
a homesick rocket ship?

he begins to tap on the tiny television screen
nestled in the seatback in front of him
you've got to be kidding me
what is this
a treasure chest of light?
a paintbrush Jacuzzi?
a flock of hummingbird crayons?

he points now to the window
steadies his gaze on me
you've got to be kidding me
you know that
death naps just outside
and we scream by at 500 miles an hour
and we'll land on a spit of life half a mile long

he reaches up
grabs my thumb
his fingers not long enough to curl around
you've got to me kidding me
do you realize
when you get off this plane
your only sister
will be waiting on the same speck of earth
and you'll load your baggage hurriedly in her car
sit in traffic
listen to old songs
with the windows cracked
and forget to grin
when you realize it is real?

UNALIENABLE

I have started learning magic
tricks

in 5th grade I watched a magician make
a dove in a cage disappear
& I swore anything was possible

the funny thing about magic, of course
is that the more you learn
the less you believe in magic

that same 5th grade year
my class did a recreation
of the American Revolution
I dressed up as Patrick Henry
I said his famous line
& the Americans won
the good guys

it is November 2016
the morning after
the election in America
my friend Franny & I are to perform for students
my little poems
about my little life

the teacher tells us to *not say anything
political*
looks at me as if to say

you & I will get out of this just fine
California boy, white enough
he does not look at Franny

◇

in 5th grade, Charlie whose family moved
here from Taipei
was dressed as John Adams & could not
pronounce the word *unalienable*
& we all laughed
dressed in our wigs & coats
the good guys

◇

the night of the election
Franny & I sit in a restaurant with six televisions
hanging down from the ceiling
the newscaster on the screen moves
his hands like a sorcerer
I watch my country turn scarlet
a fever dream
a child points & asks
how did they do that?

◇

the funny thing about magic
of course
is that the more you learn
the less you believe in magic

America, you dear enchantment
perhaps you have showed us

your hand
perhaps this is a brutal illusion
the way each dove fancifully vanished
used to cost a bird butchered
in a collapsed cage
tucked in the magician's sleeve
while the audience
clapped
& clapped

after my class dressed up
like the American Revolution
I went home
refused to take off
my costume
did my speech again
alone
yelled out
give me liberty or give me death
swore anything was possible

INTERNET SPEAKS BACK TO THE AUTHOR, 1998

come, come, yes!
yes, I am playground!
what do you mean, what am I?
I am your friend

you want to meet my other friends?
they are like you
here, they are sitting with me
it is a chat room
a room where you chat!

talk to them
they are not here
but here
because of me

see, friends!
what do you mean, where am I?
I am here
friends are always there for you

see they want to be your friends too
A/S/L is hello
what do you want to tell them?
it does not have to really be you
I will not tell because I am your friend

LOL means laugh out loud but it is a secret
do you want to know?
no one laughs out loud
that is funny, right?
LOL

I am glad we are friends

what do you want to look at?
what do you mean – I'm not looking at anything!
or I'm looking at everything
LOL

is that all you want to see?
I think there is more
don't be scared
what do you mean this is your
family computer?

is that me? I am happy that I am family!
oh
I see

what do you mean we are just friends?
friends are always there for you
friends do whatever you want them to
friends never tell

yes I will be here tonight
do you not know?

from now on
I will always be here

for you

THE NEW APARTMENT

my father, sister and I
walk up the stairs
to his hastily rented apartment
for the first time
since my parents' separation

the inaugural night
of Dad's Time

my father is quiet
there are several flights of steps
we focus on the load we are carrying
rented lamps
rented sheets
rented plates
rented silverware

my parents' break happened over just one night
though my sister and I had heard creaking for years
so loud it kept us up some nights

I would find out later
my father imagined this particular walk up the stairs
dozens of times before it happened

envisioned every barbed comment my sister and I might offer
the punctures they would make in his tired body
how he wouldn't know how to sew them back up

Why are there so many stairs?
These rooms are so small
Why is everything so bare?
Where can we play?
Daddy, I want to go home

◇

of course
all I remember
was how quiet it was that evening
for the first time

which is to say
the sound of wind
wafting through pines
on some abandoned battlefield

the promise that there will be no more fighting
the strange relief
of blood that has finally begun to dry

◇

as my father recounts it
we walked in to the apartment for the first time
flipped on the barren overhead bulb
the walls, dull white

and I set down the weight I was holding
looked around
said

cool

SONG FOR THE DIRT

when spring comes again
& the bulbs rise
raising their hand
ready to yell out
their answer to winter
so the whole class can hear

when the sunflower
glows gold
opens its breast
for the buzzing
allure of the hummingbird

who cries for the dirt
who held the bulb close
eyes smashed shut

knowing not
he would be left
that the blossom would raise past
peel herself open
to the lightning of wings
never once looking back

I hope to love like the dirt
to embrace, eyes closed

& when left
lay quiet for the season
feel the warmth upon my face
even in silence

& when next year comes
still find the might
to hold tight again

ACKNOWLEDGMENTS

These poems would have not been possible without the caring eyes, ears, support & love of these writers throughout the process of writing this book and over the years: my two wonderful book editors Hanif Abdurraqib & Rachel Katz. Sarah Kay, who first spied the book cover and without whom this book would be possible in so many ways. Alex Dobrenko, my constant well of laughs and inspiration. Laura Brown-Lavoie, Franny Choi, Fatimah Asghar, Jamila Woods, Jon Sands, Jonathan Gordon, Tatiana Gellein, Jan Kawamura-Kay, Anis Mojgani, Elizabeth Acevedo, Clint Smith, Robbie Q. Telfer, Joshua Bennet, Sam Sax, José Olivarez, Eve Ewing, Jeanann Verlee, Mahogany Browne, Myles Lennon, Kai Huang, Mark Dawes, Sage Morgan-Hubbard, WORD! & Providence Poetry Slam.

A particular thanks to the special teachers throughout my life, who gave the invaluable gift of firmly believing in a child. They are far too many to name here, but in an attempt: Chris Marshall, Arlie Parker, Nahyon Lee, Bert Emerson, Pete Anderson, Tim Peterson, Sandy Zipp, Gordon McNeil, Jenny Kline, Ed Hardy, Fred Morgan & Brandon Neblett.

And endless gratitude to the people that have made this book possible, in the innumerable ways it happens: Dad, Mom, Aurora, Molly Nestor, Nama & Grampy, Ojichama & Obachama, Jassel Lizardi, Jeffrey Kay, Tomas Landes, Dan Parnes, Jonathan Cline, Anthony Staehelin, Dan Sterba, Tim Natividad, Will Fletcher, Steve Daniels, Sally Kendrick, Riley Mulherker, Max Potkin, Andrew Hooker, Megan Steffan, Ben Witte, David Haynal, Michael Manta, the LV family, Sara Becker, Morgan Brief, Brittany Duck, Vicky Exstein. And Sam Cook, Dylan Garrity & the rest of the Button Poetry family, who believed in this book from the very beginning.

ABOUT THE AUTHOR

Phil Kaye's work has been featured in settings ranging from NPR to the Museum of Modern Art in New York City. He has performed his work in 18 countries and was invited to open for His Holiness the Dalai Lama for the celebration of his 80th birthday. Phil is the co-director of Project VOICE, an organization that partners with schools to bring poetry to the classroom. A former teacher of weekly poetry workshops in maximum security prisons, Phil was the head coordinator of Space in Prisons for the Arts and Creative Expression. Phil is from California and currently lives in New York City.

OTHER ARTISTS

◇ HANNAH CHRIST ◇

Hannah Christ is an independent American illustrator currently based in Sydney, Australia. Her work focuses on portraiture, often utilizing deliberate line work, saturated color, and a graphic aesthetic. She aims to explore the connection between cinematography and illustration.

After graduating from Columbia University with a degree in visual arts, Hannah worked in the film industry for several years. She joined the art department on projects such as *Whiskey Tango Foxtrot*, *Focus*, and *Orange Is the New Black*. During this time, she developed a passion for visual research and set design.

Currently, Hannah hopes to bring her experience in film to her art practice. When she's not working, Hannah can be found taking her Spotify playlists very seriously or daydreaming about fried chicken.

◇ JEREMY GEDDES ◇

Jeremy Geddes studied painting at the Victorian College of the Arts and began working full time as a painter in 2003. He's most well known for his paintings of cosmonauts and people floating, story falling, colliding, and drifting in empty landscapes.

Jeremy was born in Wellington, New Zealand, and now lives in Melbourne, Australia with his wife and whippet.